I0425868

This publication has been developed by the
U.S. Department of Labor, Employee Benefits
Security Administration (EBSA).

To view this and other publications, visit the
agency's website at: **www.dol.gov/ebsa**.
To order publications, contact us electronically
at: **www.askebsa.dol.gov**.
Or call toll free: **1-866-444-3272**.

For assistance from a benefits advisor, visit EBSA's website
at **www.dol.gov/ebsa** and click on "Request Assistance."
Or call toll free: **1-866-444-3272**.

This material will be made available in alternative format
to persons with disabilities upon request:

Voice phone: (202) 693-8664
TTY: (202) 501-3911

WHAT YOU SHOULD KNOW ABOUT YOUR RETIREMENT

▶ TABLE OF CONTENTS

▶ Introduction

Your employer's retirement savings plan is an essential part of your future financial security. It is important to understand how your plan works and what benefits you will receive. Just as you would keep track of money that you put in a bank or other financial institution, it is in your best interest to keep track of your retirement benefits.

Those responsible for the management and oversight of your retirement plan must follow certain rules for operating the plan, handling the plan's money, and overseeing the firms that manage the money. You should also understand and monitor your retirement plan and your benefits. You will find **Action Items** in each chapter to assist you in doing this.

This booklet helps you understand your plan and explains what information you should review periodically and where to go for help with questions. It includes information on:

- ▶ Different types of retirement plans;
- ▶ What information you can get about your plan;
- ▶ When and how you can receive retirement benefits;
- ▶ What to do if you have a question or find a mistake;
- ▶ The responsibilities of those who manage the plan and its investments;
- ▶ Your responsibilities to understand and monitor your plan; and
- ▶ Specific circumstances such as how a divorce or change of employer ownership may affect your retirement benefit.

Any terms you see that appear in **blue** in the text are explained in the Glossary.

Retirement plans covered in this booklet

This booklet covers private retirement plans that are governed by Federal laws and guidelines in the **Employee Retirement Income Security Act of 1974 (ERISA)** and the Internal Revenue Code. ERISA is a Federal statute that sets standards for most employer and union sponsored retirement plans in private industry and imposes responsibilities on those running the plan. Participants in these plans have certain rights as well as responsibilities.

The rules discussed in this booklet do **not** apply to all retirement plans. For example, the information does not apply to:

- ▶ State and local government plans, including plans covering public school teachers and school administrators;
- ▶ Most church plans; and
- ▶ Plans for Federal government employees.

Also, if you are in a collectively bargained plan, the rules that apply under ERISA may be different in some cases.

The information contained in the following pages answers the most common questions about retirement plans. Keep in mind, however, that this booklet is a simplified summary of participant rights and responsibilities, not a legal interpretation of ERISA.

▶ CHAPTER 1: TYPES OF RETIREMENT PLANS

The first step to understanding your retirement benefits is to find out what kind of retirement plan your employer has. There are two major types of plans, defined benefit and defined contribution, which are described here and outlined in Table 1 on page 4. Keep in mind that your employer may have more than one type of plan, and may have different participation requirements for each.

A **defined benefit plan**, funded by the employer, promises you a specific monthly benefit at retirement. The plan may state this promised benefit as an exact dollar amount, such as $100 per month at retirement. Or, more often, it may calculate your benefit through a formula that includes factors such as your salary, your age, and the number of years you worked at the company. For example, your pension benefit might be equal to 1 percent of your average salary for the last 5 years of employment times your total years of service.

A **defined contribution plan**, on the other hand, does not promise you a specific benefit amount at retirement. Instead, you and/or your employer contribute money to your individual account in the plan. In many cases, you are responsible for choosing how these contributions are invested, and deciding how much to contribute from your paycheck through pretax deductions. Your employer may add to your account, in some cases by matching a certain percentage of your contributions. The value of your account depends on how much is contributed and how well the investments perform. At retirement, you receive the balance in your account, reflecting the contributions, investment gains or losses, and any fees charged against your account. The **401(k) plan** is a popular type of defined contribution plan. There are four types of 401(k) plans: traditional 401(k), **safe harbor 401(k)**, **SIMPLE 401(k)**, and **automatic enrollment** 401(k) plans. The **SIMPLE IRA plan**, **SEP**, **employee stock ownership plan (ESOP)**, and **profit sharing plan** are other examples of defined contribution plans. (See explanations of the various types of plans in the Glossary at the end.)

NOTE

1. Employers can choose whether to offer a retirement plan to employees; Federal law does not require employers to offer or to continue to offer a plan.
2. The Pension Benefit Guaranty Corporation (PBGC) guarantees payment of certain retirement benefits for participants in most private defined benefit plans if the plan is terminated without enough money to pay all of the promised benefits. The government does not guarantee benefit payments for defined contribution plans. For more information, see the PBGC's website at **www.pbgc.gov**.
3. Some hybrid plans – such as **cash balance plans** – contain features of both types of plans described above. See the Glossary for information on this type of plan.

ACTION ITEM

Ask your plan administrator, human resources office or employer for information on what type of plan or plans you have at work. You can ask for a copy of the **Summary Plan Description** (the retirement plan booklet that you should receive when you enroll in the plan) and review the information about the plan.

Table 1: Characteristics of Def ned Benef t and Def ned Contribution Plans

	Def ned Benef t Plan	Def ned Contribution Plan
Employer Contributions and/or Matching Contributions	Employer funded. Federal rules set amounts that employers must contribute to plans in an effort to ensure that plans have enough money to pay benefits when due. There are penalties for failing to meet these requirements.	There is no requirement that the employer contribute, except in SIMPLE and safe harbor 401(k)s, money purchase plans, SIMPLE IRAs, and SEPs. The employer may have to contribute in certain automatic enrollment 401(k) plans. The employer may choose to match a portion of the employee's contributions or to contribute without employee contributions. In some plans, employer contributions may be in the form of employer stock.
Employee Contributions	Generally, employees do not contribute to these plans.	Many plans require the employee to contribute in order for an account to be established.
Managing the Investment	Plan officials manage the investment and the employer is responsible for ensuring that the amount it has put in the plan plus investment earnings will be enough to pay the promised benefit.	The employee often is responsible for managing the investment of his or her account, choosing from investment options offered by the plan. In some plans, plan officials are responsible for investing all the plan's assets.
Amount of Benef ts Paid Upon Retirement	A promised benefit is based on a formula in the plan, often using a combination of the employee's age, years worked for the employer, and/or salary.	The benefit depends on contributions made by the employee and/or the employer, performance of the account's investments, and fees charged to the account.
Type of Retirement Benef t Payments	Traditionally, these plans pay the retiree monthly annuity payments that continue for life. Plans may offer other payment options.	The retiree may transfer the account balance into an individual retirement account (IRA) from which the retiree withdraws money, or may receive it as a lump sum payment. Some plans also offer monthly payments through an annuity.
Guarantee of Benef ts	The Federal Government, through the Pension Benefit Guaranty Corporation (PBGC), guarantees some amount of benefits.	No Federal guarantee of benefits.
Leaving the Company Before Retirement Age	If an employee leaves after vesting in a benefit but before the plan's retirement age, the benefit generally stays with the plan until the employee files a claim for it at retirement. Some defined benefit plans offer early retirement options.	The employee may transfer the account balance to an individual retirement account (IRA) or, in some cases, another employer plan, where it can continue to grow based on investment earnings. The employee also may take the balance out of the plan, but will owe taxes and possibly penalties, thus reducing retirement income. Plans may cash out small accounts.

▷ CHAPTER 2: EARNING RETIREMENT BENEFITS

Once you have learned what type of retirement plan your employer offers, you need to find out when you can participate in the plan and begin to earn benefits. Plan rules can vary as long as they meet the requirements under Federal law. You need to check with your plan or review the plan booklet (called the **Summary Plan Description**) to learn your plan's rules and requirements. Your plan may require you to work for the company for a period of time before you may participate in the plan. In addition, there typically is a time frame for when you begin to accumulate benefits and earn the right to them (sometimes referred to as "**vesting**").

WHO CAN PARTICIPATE IN YOUR EMPLOYER'S RETIREMENT PLAN?

Find out if you are within the group of employees covered by your employer's retirement plan. Federal law allows employers to include certain groups of employees and exclude others from a retirement plan. For example, your employer may sponsor one plan for salaried employees and another for union employees. Part-time employees may be eligible if they work at least 1,000 hours per year, which is about 20 hours per week. So if you work part-time, find out if you are covered.

WHEN CAN YOUR PARTICIPATION BEGIN?

Once you know you are covered, you need to find out when you can begin to participate in the plan. You can find this information in your plan's Summary Plan Description. Federal law sets minimum requirements, but a plan may be more generous. Generally, a plan may require an employee to be at least 21 years old and to have a **year of service** with the company before the employee can participate in a plan. However, plans may allow employees to begin participation before reaching age 21 or completing one year of service. For administrative reasons, your participation may be delayed up to 6 months after you meet these age and service criteria, or until the start of the next **plan year**, whichever is sooner. The plan year is the calendar year, or an alternative 12-month period, that a retirement plan uses for plan administration. Because the rules can vary, it is important that you learn the rules for your plan.

Employers have some flexibility to require additional years of service in some circumstances. For example, if your plan allows you to vest (discussed in detail later in this chapter) immediately upon participating in the plan, it may require that you work for the company for two years before you may participate in the plan.

Federal law also imposes other participation rules for certain circumstances. For example, if you were an older worker when you were hired, you cannot be excluded from participating in the plan just because you are close to retirement age.

Some **401(k) plans** and **SIMPLE IRA plans** enroll employees automatically. This means that you will automatically become a participant in the plan unless you choose to opt out. The plan will deduct a set contribution level from your paycheck and put it into a predetermined investment. If your employer has an automatic enrollment plan, you should receive a notice describing the automatic contribution process, when your participation begins, your opportunity to opt out of the plan or change your contribution level and where your automatic contributions are invested. If you are in a 401(k), the notice will also describe your right to change investments, or if you are in a SIMPLE IRA plan, your right to change the financial institution where your contributions are invested.

WHEN DO YOU BEGIN TO ACCUMULATE BENEFITS?

Once you begin to participate in a retirement plan, you need to understand how you accrue or earn benefits. Your accrued benefit is the amount of retirement benefits that you have accumulated or that have been allocated to you under the plan at any particular point in time.

Defined benefit plans often count your years of service in order to determine whether you have earned a benefit and also to calculate how much you will receive in benefits at retirement. Employees in the plan who work part-time, but who work 1,000 hours or more each year, must be credited with a portion of the benefit in proportion to what they would have earned if they were employed full time. In a **defined contribution plan**, your **benefit accrual** is the amount of contributions and earnings that have accumulated in your 401(k) or other retirement plan account, minus any fees charged to your account by your plan.

Special rules for when you begin to accumulate benefits may apply to certain types of retirement plans. For example, in a **Simplified Employee Pension Plan (SEP)**, all participants who earn at least $550 a year from their employers are entitled to receive a contribution.

CAN A PLAN REDUCE PROMISED BENEFITS?

Defined benefit plans may change the rate at which you earn future benefits but cannot reduce the amount of benefits you have already accumulated. For example, a plan that accrues benefits at the rate of $5 a month for years of service through 2011 may be amended to provide that for years of service beginning in 2012 benefits will be credited at the rate of $4 per month. Plans that make a significant reduction in the rate at which benefits accumulate must provide you with written notice generally at least 45 days before the change goes into effect.

Also, in most situations, if a company terminates a defined benefit plan that does not have enough funding to pay all of the promised benefits, the Pension Benefit Guaranty Corporation (PBGC) will pay plan participants and beneficiaries some retirement benefits, but possibly less than the level of benefits promised. (For more information, see the PBGC's website at **www.pbgc.gov**.)

In a defined contribution plan, the employer may change the amount of employer contributions in the future. Depending on the plan terms, the employer may also be able to stop making contributions for a few years or indefinitely.

An employer may terminate a defined benefit or a defined contribution plan, but may not reduce the benefit you have already accrued in the plan.

HOW SOON DO YOU HAVE A RIGHT TO YOUR ACCUMULATED BENEFITS?

You immediately vest in your own contributions and the earnings on them. This means you have earned the right to these amounts without the risk of forfeiting them. But note – there are restrictions on actually taking them out of the plan. See the discussion on the rules for distributions later in this booklet.

However, you do not necessarily have an immediate right to any contributions made by your employer. Federal law provides a maximum number of years a company may require employees to work to earn the vested right to all or some of these benefits. (See tables on pages 8-9 showing the vesting rules.)

In a defined benefit plan, an employer can require that employees have 5 years of service in order to become 100 percent vested in the employer funded benefits (called cliff vesting). Employers also can choose a graduated vesting schedule, which requires an employee to work 7 years in order to be 100 percent vested, but provides at least 20 percent vesting after 3 years, 40 percent after 4 years, 60 percent after 5 years, and 80 percent after 6 years of service. The permitted vesting schedules for current defined benefit plans are shown in Table 3 on page

9. Plans may provide a different schedule as long as it is more generous than these vesting schedules. (Unlike most defined benefit plans, in a cash balance plan, employees vest in employer contributions after 3 years.)

In a defined contribution plan such as a 401(k) plan, you are always 100 percent vested in your own contributions to a plan, and in any subsequent earnings from your contributions. However, in most defined contribution plans you may have to work several years before you are vested in the employer's matching contributions. (There are exceptions, such as the SIMPLE 401(k) and safe harbor 401(k), in which you are immediately vested in all required employer contributions. You also vest immediately in the SIMPLE IRA and the SEP.)

Currently, employers have a choice of two different vesting schedules for employer matching 401(k) contributions, which are shown in Table 2 on page 8. Your employer may use a schedule in which employees are 100 percent vested in employer contributions after 3 years of service (cliff vesting). Under graduated vesting, an employee must be at least 20 percent vested after 2 years, 40 percent after 3 years, 60 percent after 4 years, 80 percent after 5 years, and 100 percent after 6 years. If your automatic enrollment 401(k) plan requires employer contributions, you vest in those contributions after 2 years. Automatic enrollment 401(k) plans with optional matching contributions follow one of the vesting schedules noted above.

Employers making other contributions to defined contribution plans, such as a 401(k) plan, also can choose between two vesting schedules. For those contributions made since 2007, they can choose between the graduated and cliff vesting schedules in Table 2. For contributions made prior to 2007, they can choose between the schedules provided in Table 3.

You may lose some of the employer-provided benefits you have earned if you leave your job before you have worked long enough to be vested. However, once vested, you have the right to receive the vested portion of your benefits even if you leave your job before retirement. But even though you have the right to certain benefits, your defined contribution plan account value could decrease after you leave your job as a result of investment performance.

NOTE

If you leave your company and return, you may be able to count your earlier period of employment towards the years of service needed for vesting in the employer-provided benefits. Unless your break in service with the company was 5 years or a time equal to the length of your pre-break employment, whichever is greater, you likely can count that time prior to your break. Because these rules are very specific, you should read your plan document carefully if you are contemplating a short-term break from your employer, and then discuss it with your plan administrator. If you left employment prior to January 1, 1985, different rules apply. For more information, contact the Department of Labor electronically by visiting the website at **www.dol.gov/ebsa** and clicking on "Request Assistance" or by calling toll free 1-866-444-3272.

For Reserve and National Guard units called to active duty, the Uniformed Services Employment and Reemployment Rights Act (USERRA) requires that the period of military duty be counted as covered service with the employer for eligibility, vesting, and benefit accrual purposes. Returning service members are treated as if they had been continuously employed regardless of the type of retirement plan the employer has adopted. However, a person who is reemployed is entitled to accrued benefits resulting from employee contributions only to the extent that he or she actually makes the contributions to the plan.

Vesting Rules
Generally, an employer must count your years of service for vesting credit starting with your date of employment. Two exceptions provide that your employer may start counting your years of service with the first plan year following (1) your 18th birthday if you were under 18 years of age when you started working there, and (2) the date you start contributing to a 401(k) plan if you elected not to contribute when you first were eligible. Plans can allow employees the right to employer-provided benefits sooner than indicated in the following tables.

MINIMUM VESTING REQUIREMENTS UNDER ERISA
EMPLOYER CONTRIBUTIONS
(USE TABLE IN EFFECT ON DATE YOU LEFT EMPLOYER)

Table 2 below shows the current vesting schedules, as of 2002, for employer matching 401(k) plan contributions, and for other employer contributions to a defined contribution plan as of 2007.

TABLE 2: Effective Date 1/01/02 - Present — for 401(k) Matching Contributions Effective Date 1/01/07 – Present — for Other Def ned Contribution Employer Contributions	
GRADUATED VESTING	
Years of Service	Non-forfeitable Percentage
2	20%
3	40%
4	60%
5	80%
6	100%
Cliff Vesting Less than 3 years of service - 0% Vested At least 3 years of service - 100% Vested	

Table 3 is for employees in a defined benefit plan. It is also for employees receiving other employer contributions to a defined contribution plan before 2007*, employer matching 401(k) contributions prior to 2002, and employees in a defined contribution plan who left an employer after December 31, 1988.

* If your plan is top heavy, Table 2 applies.

TABLE 3: Effective Date 1/01/89 – Present* — for Def ned Benef t Employer Contributions Effective Date 1/01/89 – 2007 — for Other Def ned Contribution Employer Contributions Effective Date 1/01/89 – 2002 — 401(k) Matching Employer Contributions	
GRADUATED VESTING	
Years of Service	**Non-forfeitable Percentage**
3	20%
4	40%
5	60%
6	80%
7	100%
Cliff Vesting Less than 5 years of service - 0% Vested At least 5 years of service - 100% Vested	

Table 4 is for employees who left before 1989.

TABLE 4: Effective Date 1974 - 12/31/88** — for all Def ned Benef t and Def ned Contribution Employer Contributions	
GRADUATED VESTING	
Years of Service	**Non-forfeitable Percentage**
5	25%
6	30%
7	35%
8	40%
9	45%
10	50%
11	60%
12	70%
13	80%
14	90%
15	100%
Cliff Vesting Less than 10 years of service - 0% Vested At least 10 years of service - 100% Vested	
Rule of 45 If employee's age and years of service total 45, and the employee has at least 5 years of service, then 50% of the benefits must be vested, with at least 10% vesting for each year thereafter.	

Note

For plans subject to collective bargaining agreements, the effective date is the earlier of the date on which the last of the collective bargaining agreements under which the plan is maintained terminates or —
* 01/01/99.
**01/01/89.

Action Items

► Find out if you are covered by an employer plan.
► Find out how soon you can start participating in and/or contributing to your retirement plan after you start working for a company.
► Get a Summary Plan Description.
► Review your plan document or Summary Plan Description to understand how you earn benefits in your plan.
► Find your plan's vesting schedule to check when you are fully vested. If you are thinking of changing jobs, check your plan to see if working longer will allow you to vest more fully in your employer's contributions.

▶ CHAPTER 3: PLAN INFORMATION TO REVIEW

If you have a question about your retirement plan, you can start by looking for an answer in the information that the plan provides. You can request this information from your **plan administrator**, the person who is in charge of running the plan. Your employer can tell you how to contact your plan administrator.

INFORMATION PROVIDED BY THE RETIREMENT PLAN

Each retirement plan is required to have a formal, written **plan document** that details how it operates and its requirements. As noted previously, there is also a booklet that describes the key plan rules, called the **Summary Plan Description (SPD)**, which should be much easier to read and understand. The SPD also should include a summary of any material changes to the plan or to the information required to be in the SPD. In many cases, you can start with the SPD and then look at the plan document if you still have questions.

In addition, plans must provide you with a number of notices. Some of the key notices are described in Table 5 on page 12.

For example, **defined contribution plans**, such as **401(k) plans**, generally are required to provide advance notice to employees when a "blackout period" occurs. A blackout period is when a participant's right to direct investments, take loans, or obtain distributions is suspended for a period of at least three consecutive business days. Blackout periods can often occur when plans change recordkeepers or investment options.

Some plan information, such as the Summary Plan Description, must be provided to you automatically and without charge at the time periods indicated below. You may request a Summary Plan Description at other times, but your employer might charge you a copying fee. You must ask the plan if you want other information, such as a copy of the written plan document or the plan's Form 5500 annual financial report, and you may have to pay a copying fee. See Table 5 on page 12 and Table 6 on page 14. Many employers provide benefit information on a website.

In some cases, plans provide information more frequently than required by Federal law. For instance, some plans allow participants to check their statements online or by telephone.

The plan's annual financial report (Form 5500) is also available. You can find the report online at **www.dol.gov/ebsa** or by contacting the U.S. Department of Labor, EBSA Public Disclosure Facility, Room N-1513, 200 Constitution Avenue, NW, Washington, D.C. 20210, telephone: (202) 693-8673. There is a copying fee if the report is over 100 pages. In addition, if your plan administrator does not provide you, as a participant covered under the plan, with a copy of the Summary Plan Description automatically or after you request it, you may contact the Department of Labor electronically by visiting the website at **www.dol.gov/ebsa** and clicking on "Request Assistance" or by calling toll free 1-866-444-3272 for help.

TABLE 5: Key Information Your Plan Administrator Must Provide Automatically

What	Description	When
Summary Plan Description (SPD)	A summary version of the plan document and other important plan information, in easier-to-understand language.	▸ Within 90 days of becoming a participant in the plan; and ▸ An updated copy every 10 years (5 years if the plan has been amended).
Automatic Enrollment Notice	For plans with automatic enrollment, a description of the automatic enrollment process, the percentage of salary being deferred, the default investment used for automatic contributions, your right to opt out of the plan, your right to change deferral percentage and investments, and how to find information about the plan's other investments.	▸ Generally, at least 30 days before you are eligible to participate; and ▸ At least 30 days before the beginning of each subsequent plan year.
Individual Benef t Statement	Statement providing information about your account balance and vested benefits. Depending on the type of plan you have, the statement may also include the value of the investments in the account and information describing your right to direct investments.	▸ At least quarterly for participant-directed defined contribution plans; ▸ At least annually for non-participant-directed defined contribution plans; or ▸ At least every 3 years for defined benefit plans.
Annual Funding Notice	Basic information about the funding status and financial condition of the defined benefit pension plan, including the plan's funding percentage; assets and liabilities; and a description of the benefits guaranteed by the PBGC.	Within 120 days of the end of the plan year.
Plan and Investment Information for Participant - Directed Plans	Plan and investment related information, including information about fees and expenses, so participants can make informed decisions to manage their individual accounts. The investment related information must be	▸ Before a participant can direct investments for the first time; ▸ At least annually thereafter; and ▸ At least quarterly for fees and expenses actually paid.

What	Description	When
	provided in a format, such as a chart, that allows for comparison among the plan's investment options.	
Summary of Material Modif cations	A summary of significant plan changes or changes in the information required to be in the SPD.	Within 7 months of the end of the plan year in which the changes were made.
Summary Annual Report	A summary of financial information filed by the plan on its Form 5500 Annual Return/Report. If your plan is required to provide an annual funding notice, your plan is not required to provide this report.	Within 9 months after the end of the plan year or 2 months after the annual report filing deadline.
Notice of Signif cant Reduction in Future Benef t Accruals	Notice of any significant reduction in the rate of future benefit accruals, or the elimination of or significant reduction in an early retirement benefit or retirement-type subsidy. Applies to defined benefit plans and certain defined contribution plans.	At least 45 days before the effective date of the plan amendment.
Blackout Notice	Notice of a period of more than 3 consecutive business days when there is a temporary suspension, limitation or restriction on directing or diversifying plan assets, obtaining loans, or obtaining distributions. Applies to most 401(k) or other individual account plans.	Generally, at least 30 days before the blackout date.
Notice to Participants of Underfunded Plan	For defined benefit plans that are less than 80% funded, the notice of the funding level of the plan and information on PBGC guarantees.	Within 2 months after the due date for filing the annual report.

TABLE 6: Key Information Your Plan Administrator Must Provide Upon Written Request

What	Description	Cost
Plan Documents	Documents that provide the terms of the plan, including collective bargaining agreements and trust agreements.	Reasonable copying charge
Annual Report (Form 5500) – most recent report	Financial information about the plan that most plans are required to file with the government within 7 months of the end of the **plan year**.	Reasonable copying charge

WHAT PLAN INFORMATION SHOULD YOU REVIEW REGULARLY?

If you are in a **defined benefit plan**, you will receive an **individual benefit statement** once every 3 years. Review its description of the total benefits you have earned and whether you are vested in those benefits. Also check to make sure your date of birth, date of hire, and the other information included is correct. You will also receive an annual notice of the plan's funding status.

Defined contribution plans, including 401(k) plans, also must send participants individual benefit statements either quarterly, if participants direct the investments of their accounts, or annually, if they do not. When you receive a statement, check it to make sure all of the information is accurate. This information may include:

- Salary level
- Amounts that you and your employer have contributed
- **Years of service** with the employer
- Home address
- Social Security Number
- Beneficiary designation
- Marital status
- The performance of your investments (defined contribution plan participants)
- Fees paid by the plan and/or charged to participants. (For more information, contact us electronically at **www.askebsa.dol.gov** or call our toll free number at 1-866-444-3272 to ask for the booklet "A Look at 401(k) Plan Fees.") Check with your plan to see if this information is included in materials on your investment options, the benefit statement, the Summary Plan Description or the plan's Annual Report (Form 5500). See Chapter 7 for more information on the fees that your employer can charge to your account.

ACTION ITEMS

- Make sure you have received the plan's Summary Plan Description and read it for information on how your plan works.
- Read other documents you receive from your plan to make sure that you keep up with any plan changes, and check that the information on your benefit statement is accurate.

- If you are in a defined contribution plan, ask for information on the investment choices available in the plan, and find out when and how you can change your plan account investments.
- If you suspect errors in your plan information, contact your plan administrator or the human resources department.
- If there have been changes in your personal information, such as a marriage, divorce or change of address, contact your plan administrator or the human resources department.
- Keep your plan documents in a safe place in case questions arise in the future.

► CHAPTER 4: PAYMENT OF BENEFITS

Once you understand what type of plan you have, how you earn benefits, and how much your benefits will be, it is important to learn when and how you can receive them.

WHEN CAN YOU BEGIN TO RECEIVE RETIREMENT BENEFITS?

There are several points to keep in mind in determining when you can receive benefits:

1. Federal law provides guidelines, shown in Table 7 below, for when plans must start paying retirement benefits.
2. Plans can choose to start paying benefits sooner. The plan documents will state when you may begin receiving payments from your plan.
3. You must file a claim for benefits for your payments to begin. This takes some time for administrative reasons. (See Chapter 6.)

TABLE 7: Requirements Under Federal Law for Payment of Retirement Benef ts		
Under Federal law, your plan must allow you to begin receiving benefits* the later of -	**Or -**	**Or -**
Reaching age 65 or the age your plan considers to be normal retirement age (if earlier)	10 years of service	Terminating your service with the employer

*For administrative reasons, benefits do not begin immediately after meeting these conditions. At a minimum, your plan must provide that you will start receiving benefits within 60 days after the end of the plan year in which you satisfy the conditions. Also, you need to file a claim under your plan's procedures. (See Chapter 6.)

Under certain circumstances, your benefit payments may be suspended if you continue to work beyond normal retirement age. The plan must notify you of the suspension during the first calendar month or payroll period in which payments are withheld. This information should also be included in the **Summary Plan Description**. A plan also must advise you of its procedures for requesting an advance determination of whether a particular type of reemployment would result in a suspension of benefit payments. If you are a retiree and are considering taking a job, you may wish to write to your plan administrator and ask if your benefits would be suspended.

Table 7 shows the general requirements for when payments begin. Listed below are some permitted variations:

► Although **defined benefit plans** and **money purchase plans** generally allow you to receive benefits only when you reach the plan's retirement age, some have provisions for early retirement.

- **401(k) plans** often allow you to receive your account balance when you leave your job.
- 401(k) plans may allow for distributions while still employed if you have reached age 59½ or if you suffer a hardship.
- **Profit sharing plans** may permit you to receive your **vested** benefit after a specific number of years or whenever you leave your job.
- A phased retirement option allows employees at or near retirement age to reduce their work hours to part-time, receive benefits, and continue to earn additional funds.
- **ESOPs** do not have to pay out any benefits until 1 year after the plan year in which you retire, or as many as 6 years if you leave for reasons other than retirement, death, or disability.

WARNING

1. You may owe current income taxes – and possibly tax penalties — on your distribution if you take money out before age 59½, unless you transfer it to an **IRA** or another tax-qualified retirement plan.
2. Taking all or a portion of your funds out of your account before retirement age will mean you have less in retirement benefits.

WHEN IS THE LATEST YOU MAY BEGIN TO TAKE PAYMENT OF YOUR BENEFITS?

Federal law sets a mandatory date by which you must start receiving your retirement benefits, even if you would like to wait longer. This mandatory start date generally is set to begin on April 1 following the calendar year in which you turn 70½ or, if later, when you retire. However, your plan may require you to begin receiving distributions even if you have not retired by age 70½.

IN WHAT FORM WILL YOUR BENEFITS BE PAID?

If you are in a defined benefit or money purchase plan, the plan must offer you a benefit in the form of a life annuity, which means that you will receive equal, periodic payments, often as a monthly benefit, which will continue for the rest of your life. Defined benefit and money purchase plans may also offer other payment options, so check with the plan. If you are in a **defined contribution plan** (other than a money purchase plan), the plan may pay your benefits in a single lump-sum payment as well as offer other options, including payments over a set period of time (such as 5 or 10 years) or an annuity with monthly lifetime payments.

If you are leaving your employer before retirement age, see the next chapter.

CAN A BENEFIT CONTINUE FOR YOUR SPOUSE SHOULD YOU DIE FIRST?

In a defined benefit or money purchase plan, unless you and your spouse choose otherwise, the form of payment will include a survivor's benefit. This survivor's benefit, called a qualified joint and survivor annuity (QJSA), will provide payments over your lifetime and your spouse's lifetime. The benefit payment that your surviving spouse receives must be at least half of the benefit payment you received during your joint lives. If you choose not to receive the survivor's benefit, both you and your spouse must receive a written explanation of the QJSA and, within certain time limits, you must make a written waiver and your spouse must sign a written consent to the alternative payment form without a survivor's benefit. Your spouse's signature must be witnessed by a notary or plan representative.

In most 401(k) plans and other defined contribution plans, the plan is written so different protections apply for surviving spouses. In general, in most defined contribution plans, if you should die before you receive your benefits, your surviving spouse will automatically receive them. If you wish to select a different beneficiary, your spouse must consent by signing a waiver, witnessed by a notary or plan representative.

If you were single when you enrolled in the plan and subsequently married, it is important that you notify your employer and/or plan administrator and change your status under the plan. If you do not have a spouse, it is important to name a beneficiary.

If you or your spouse left employment prior to January 1, 1985, different rules apply. For more information on these rules, contact the Department of Labor electronically by visiting the website at **www.dol.gov/ebsa** and clicking on "Request Assistance" or by calling toll free at 1-866-444-3272.

CAN YOU BORROW FROM YOUR 401(K) PLAN ACCOUNT?

401(k) plans are permitted to – but not required to – offer loans to participants. The loans must charge a reasonable rate of interest and be adequately secured. The plan must include a procedure for applying for the loans and the plan's policy for granting them. Loan amounts are limited to the lesser of 50 percent of your account balance or $50,000 and must be repaid within 5 years (unless the loan is used to purchase a principal residence).

CAN YOU GET A DISTRIBUTION FROM YOUR PLAN IF YOU ARE NOT YET 65 OR YOUR PLAN'S NORMAL RETIREMENT AGE BUT ARE FACING A SIGNIFICANT FINANCIAL HARDSHIP?

Again, defined contribution plans are permitted to – but not required to – provide distributions in case of hardship. Check your plan booklet to see if it does permit them and what circumstances are included as hardships.

ACTION ITEMS

- Find out when and in what form you can receive your benefits at retirement.
- Fill out the necessary forms to update information with your retirement plan.
- Notify the retirement plan of any change of address or marital status.
- Keep all documents for your records, including Summary Plan Descriptions, company memos, and individual benefit statements.
- For tax information, look at Internal Revenue Service Publication 575 *(Pension and Annuity Income)* by visiting **www.irs.gov** and clicking on "Publications".

► Chapter 5: Taking Your Retirement Benefit With You

If you leave an employer before you reach retirement age, whether or not you can take your benefits out and/or roll them into another tax-qualified plan or account will depend on what type of plan you are in.

If you leave before retirement, can you take your retirement benefit with you?

If you are in a **defined benefit plan** (other than a **cash balance plan**), you most likely will be required to leave the benefits with the retirement plan until you become eligible to receive them. As a result, it is very important that you update your personal information with the **plan administrator** regularly and keep current on any changes in your former employer's ownership or address.

If you are in a cash balance plan, you probably will have the option of transferring at least a portion of your account balance to an **individual retirement account** or to a new employer's plan.

If you leave your employer before retirement age and you are in a **defined contribution plan** (such as a **401(k) plan**), in most cases you will be able to transfer your account balance out of your employer's plan.

What choices do you have for taking your defined contribution benefits?

- ► A lump sum – you can choose to receive your benefits as a single payment from your plan, effectively cashing out your account. You may need to pay income taxes on the amount you receive, and possibly a penalty.
- ► A **rollover** to another retirement plan – you can ask your employer to transfer your account balance directly to your new employer's plan if it accepts such transfers.
- ► A rollover to an IRA – you can ask your employer to transfer your account balance directly to an individual retirement account (IRA).
- ► If your account balance is less than $5,000 when you leave the employer, the plan can make an immediate distribution without your consent. If this distribution is more than $1,000, the plan must automatically roll the funds into an IRA it selects, unless you elect to receive a lump sum payment or to roll it over into an IRA you choose. The plan must first send you a notice allowing you to make other arrangements, and it must follow rules regarding what type of IRA can be used (i.e., it cannot combine the distribution with savings you have deposited directly in an IRA). Rollovers must be made to an entity that is qualified to offer individual retirement plans. Also, the rollover IRA must have investments designed to preserve principal. The IRA provider may not charge more in fees and expenses for such plans than it would to its other individual retirement plan customers.

Please note: If you elect a lump sum payment and do not transfer the money to another retirement account (employer plan or IRA other than a Roth IRA), you will owe a tax penalty if you are under age 59½ and do not meet certain exceptions. In addition, you may have less to live on during your retirement. Transferring your retirement plan account balance to another plan or an IRA when you leave your job will protect the tax advantages of your account and preserve the benefits for retirement.

WHAT HAPPENS IF YOU LEAVE A JOB AND LATER RETURN?

If you leave an employer for whom you have worked for several years and later return, you may be able to count those earlier years toward **vesting**. Generally, a plan must preserve the service credit you have accumulated if you leave your employer and then return within five years. Service credit refers to the **years of service** that count towards vesting. Because these rules are very specific, you should read your **plan document** carefully if you are contemplating a short-term break from your employer, and then discuss it with your plan administrator. If you left employment prior to January 1, 1985, different rules apply.

If you retire and later go back to work for a former employer, you must be allowed to continue to accrue additional benefits, subject to a plan limit on the total years of service credited under the plan.

ACTION ITEMS

- ▸ If you are leaving an employer before retirement, find out whether you can roll your benefits into a new plan or into an IRA.
- ▸ If you are leaving your benefits in your former employer's plan, be sure to keep your contact information up to date with the former employer, and keep track of the employer's contact information.
- ▸ If you are considering taking your benefits out as a lump sum, find out what taxes and penalties you will owe, and make a plan on how you will replace that income in retirement.

▶ CHAPTER 6: FILING A CLAIM FOR BENEFITS

Federal retirement law requires all plans to have a reasonable written procedure for processing your benefits claim and appeal if your claim is denied. The **Summary Plan Description (SPD)** should include your plan's claims procedures. Usually, you fill out the required paperwork and submit it to the **plan administrator**, who then can tell you what your benefits will be and when they will start.

FILING A CLAIM AND FILING AN APPEAL

If there is a problem or a dispute about whether you qualify for benefits or what amount you should receive, check your plan's claims procedure. Federal law outlines the following claims procedures requirements:

- Once your claim is filed, the plan can take up to 90 days to reach a decision, or 180 days if it notifies you that it needs an extension.
- If your claim is denied, you must receive a written notice, including specific information about why your claim was denied and how to file an appeal.
- You have 60 days to request a full and fair review of your denied claim, using your plan's appeals procedure.
- The plan can take up to 60 days to review your appeal, as well as an additional 60 days if it notifies you of the need for an extension. The plan must then send a written notice telling you whether the appeal was granted or denied.
- If the appeal is denied, the written notice must tell you the reason, describe any additional appeal levels, and give you a statement regarding your rights to seek judicial review of the plan's decision.

If you believe the plan failed to follow **ERISA's** requirements, you may decide to seek legal advice if the plan denies your appeal. You also can contact the Department of Labor concerning your rights under ERISA electronically by visiting the website at **www.dol.gov/ebsa** and clicking on "Request Assistance" or by calling toll free 1-866-444-3272.

For more information on claims procedures, see the Department of Labor publication "Filing a Claim for Your Retirement Benefits," at **www.dol.gov/ebsa**. To obtain a copy, contact the Department of Labor electronically at **www.askebsa.dol.gov** or call toll free 1-866-444-3272.

ACTION ITEMS

- Contact your plan administrator to get the paperwork that you need to file a claim to start receiving retirement benefits.
- Contact the Department of Labor (EBSA) electronically by visiting the website at **www.dol.gov/ebsa** and clicking on "Request Assistance" or by calling toll free 1-866-444-3272 if you have questions about your plan or your rights under ERISA.

▷ Chapter 7: Responsibilities of Plan Fiduciaries

In every retirement plan, there are individuals or groups of people who use their own judgment or discretion in administering and managing the plan or who have the power to or actually control the plan's assets. These individuals or groups are called **plan fiduciaries**. Fiduciary status is based on the functions that the person performs for the plan, not just the person's title.

Does your plan have to identify those responsible for operating the plan?

A plan must name at least one fiduciary in the written plan document, or through a process described in the plan, as having control over the plan's operations. This fiduciary can be identified by office or by name. For some plans, it may be an administrative committee or the company's board of directors. Usually, a plan's fiduciaries will include the **trustee**, investment managers, and the **plan administrator**. The plan administrator is usually the best starting point for questions you might have about the plan.

What are the responsibilities of plan fiduciaries?

Fiduciaries have important responsibilities and are subject to certain standards of conduct because they act on behalf of the participants in the plan. These responsibilities include:

- Acting solely in the interest of plan participants and their beneficiaries, with the exclusive purpose of providing benefits to them;
- Carrying out their duties with skill, prudence, and diligence;
- Following the **plan documents** (unless inconsistent with **ERISA**);
- Diversifying plan investments;
- Paying only reasonable expenses of administering the plan and investing its assets; and
- Avoiding conflicts of interest.

The fiduciary also is responsible for selecting the investment providers and the investment options, and for monitoring their performance. Some plans, such as most **401(k)** or **profit sharing plans**, can be set up to permit participants to choose the investments in their accounts (within certain investment options provided by the plan). If the plan is properly set up to give participants control over their investments, then the fiduciary is not liable for losses resulting from the participant's investment decisions. Department of Labor rules provide guidance designed to make sure participants have sufficient information on the specifics of their investment options so they can make informed decisions. This information includes:

- A description of each investment option, including the investment goals, risk, and return characteristics;
- Information about any designated investment managers;
- An explanation of when and how to request changes in investments, plus any restrictions on when you can change investments;

- A statement of the fees that may be charged to your account when you change investment options or buy and sell investments; and
- The name, address, and telephone number of the plan fiduciary or other person designated to provide certain additional information on request.

A statement that the plan is intended to follow the Department of Labor rules and that the fiduciaries may be relieved of liability for losses that are the direct and necessary result of a participant's investment instructions also must be included.

For an **automatic enrollment** plan, such as an automatic enrollment **401(k) plan**, the plan fiduciary selects the investments for employees' automatic contributions if the employees do not provide direction. If the plan is properly set up, using certain default investments that generally minimize the risk of large losses and provide long-term growth, and providing notice of the plan's automatic enrollment process, then the fiduciary may be relieved of liability for losses resulting from investing in these default alternatives for participants. The plan also must provide a broad range of investments for participants to choose from and information on the plan's investments so participants can make informed decisions. Department of Labor rules provide guidance on the default investment alternatives that can be used and the notice and information to be provided to participants.

WHAT IF A PLAN FIDUCIARY FAILS TO CARRY OUT ITS RESPONSIBILITIES?

Fiduciaries that do not follow the required standards of conduct may be personally liable. If the plan lost money because of a breach of their duties, fiduciaries would have to restore those losses, or any profits received through their improper actions. For example, if an employer did not forward participants' 401(k) contributions to the plan, they would have to pay back the contributions to the plan as well as any lost earnings, and return any profits they improperly received. Fiduciaries also can be removed from their positions as fiduciaries if they fail to follow the standards of conduct.

WHEN DOES THE EMPLOYER NEED TO DEPOSIT EMPLOYEE CONTRIBUTIONS IN THE PLAN?

If you contribute to your retirement plan through deductions from your paycheck, then the employer must follow certain rules to make sure that it deposits the contributions in a timely manner. The law says that the employer must deposit participant contributions as soon as it is reasonably possible to separate them from the company's assets, but no later than the 15th business day of the month following the payday. For small plans (those with fewer than 100 participants), salary reduction contributions deposited with the plan no later than the 7th business day following withholding by the employer will be considered contributed in compliance with the law. In the Annual Report (Form 5500), the plan administrator is required to include information on whether deposits of contributions were made on a timely basis. For more information, see the Department of Labor's "Ten Warning Signs That Your 401(k) Contributions Are Being Misused," at **www.dol.gov/ebsa** for indicators of possible delays in depositing contributions.

WHAT ARE THE PLAN FIDUCIARIES' OBLIGATIONS REGARDING THE FEES AND EXPENSES PAID BY THE PLAN? CAN THE PLAN CHARGE MY DEFINED CONTRIBUTION PLAN ACCOUNT FOR FEES?

Plan fiduciaries have a specific obligation to consider the fees and expenses paid by your plan for its operations. ERISA's fiduciary standards, discussed above, mean that fiduciaries must establish a prudent process for selecting investment alternatives and service providers to the plan; ensure that fees paid to service providers and other expenses of the plan are reasonable in light of the level and quality of services provided; select investment alternatives that are prudent and adequately diversified; and monitor investment alternatives and service providers once selected to see that they continue to be appropriate choices.

The plan may deduct fees from your **defined contribution plan** account. Plan administration fees and investment fees can be deducted from your account either as a direct charge or indirectly as a reduction of your account's investment returns. Fees for individual services, such as for processing a loan from the plan or a Qualified Domestic Relations Order (see Chapter 9), also may be charged to your account.

If you direct the investments in your account, your plan will provide information about your rights and responsibilities under the plan related to directing your investments. This includes plan and investment related information, including information about fees and expenses, that you need to make informed decisions about the management of your account. The investment related information is provided in a format, such as a chart, that allows for a comparison among the plan's investment options. The plan should provide this information before you can direct investments for the first time and annually thereafter with information on the fees and expenses actually paid provided at least quarterly.

For more information, see the Department of Labor brochure "A Look at 401(k) Plan Fees" at **www.dol.gov/ebsa**. To obtain a copy, contact the Department of Labor electronically at **www.askebsa.dol.gov** or call toll free at 1-866-444-3272.

ACTION ITEM

If you have any questions about the management of the plan and its assets, contact your plan administrator.

CHAPTER 8: YOUR BENEFIT DURING A PLAN TERMINATION OR COMPANY MERGER

As noted at the beginning of this booklet, employers are not required to offer a retirement plan and plans can be modified and/or terminated.

WHAT HAPPENS WHEN A PLAN IS TERMINATED?

Federal law provides some measures to protect employees who participated in plans that are terminated, both **defined benefit** and **defined contribution**. When a plan is terminated, the current employees must become 100 percent **vested** in their accrued benefits. This means you have a right to all the benefits that you have earned at the time of the plan termination, even benefits in which you were not vested and would have lost if you had left the employer. If there is a partial termination of a plan (for example, if your employer closes a particular plant or division that results in the end of employment of a substantial percentage of plan participants) the affected employees must be immediately 100 percent vested to the extent the plan is funded.

WHAT IF YOUR TERMINATED DEFINED BENEFIT PLAN DOES NOT HAVE ENOUGH MONEY TO PAY THE BENEFITS?

The Federal Government, through the Pension Benefit Guaranty Corporation (PBGC), insures most private defined benefit plans. For terminated defined benefit plans with insufficient money to pay all of the benefits, the PBGC will guarantee the payment of your vested pension benefits up to the limits set by law. For further information on plan termination guarantees, contact the Pension Benefit Guaranty Corporation toll free at 1-800-400-7242, or visit the website at **www.pbgc.gov**.

WHAT HAPPENS IF A DEFINED CONTRIBUTION PLAN IS TERMINATED?

The PBGC does not guarantee benefits for defined contribution plans. If you are in a defined contribution plan that is in the process of terminating, the **plan fiduciaries** and **trustees** should take actions to maintain the plan until they terminate it and pay out the assets.

IS YOUR ACCRUED BENEFIT PROTECTED IF YOUR PLAN MERGES WITH ANOTHER PLAN?

Your plan rules and investment choices are likely to change if your company merges with another. Your employer may choose to merge your plan with another plan. If your plan is terminated as a result of the merger, the benefits that you have accrued cannot be reduced. You must receive a benefit that is at least equal to the benefit you were entitled to before the merger. In a defined contribution plan, the value of your account may still fluctuate after the merger based on the performance of the investments.

Special rules apply to mergers of **multiemployer defined benefit plans**, which generally are under the jurisdiction of the PBGC. Contact the PBGC for further information.

WHAT IF YOUR EMPLOYER GOES BANKRUPT?

Generally, your retirement assets should not be at risk if your employer declares bankruptcy. Federal law requires that retirement plans fund promised benefits adequately and keep plan assets separate from the employer's business assets. The funds must be held in trust or invested in an insurance contract. The employers' creditors cannot make a claim on retirement plan funds. However, it is a good idea to confirm that any contributions your employer deducts from your paycheck are forwarded to the plan's trust or insurance contract in a timely manner.

Significant business events such as bankruptcies, mergers, and acquisitions can result in employers abandoning their individual account plans (e.g., **401(k) plans**), leaving no plan fiduciary to manage it. In this situation, participants often have great difficulty in accessing the benefits they have earned and have no one to contact with questions. Custodians such as banks, insurers, and mutual fund companies are left holding the assets of these plans but do not have the authority to terminate the plans and distribute the assets. In response, the Department of Labor issued rules to create a voluntary process for the custodian to wind up the plan's business so that benefit distributions can be made and the plan terminated. Information about this program can be found on the Department of Labor's website at **www.dol.gov/ebsa**.

ACTION ITEMS

- If your former employer has gone out of business, arrangements should have been made so a plan official remains responsible for the payment of benefits and other plan business. If you are entitled to benefits and are unable to contact the **plan administrator**, contact EBSA electronically by visiting the website at **www.dol.gov/ebsa** and clicking on "Request Assistance" or by calling toll free 1-866-444-3272.
- Keep a file with information on your plan and company. If the company no longer exists under its former name, you might find some information on the Internet by entering the former name in a search engine. If your plan is abandoned, use the search function on the EBSA website, at **www.dol.gov/ebsa**, to find out if the plan's custodian is terminating the plan and the custodian's contact information.
- If your plan merges, make sure you read the communications about changes in your plan, including changes in benefits and investment choices.
- If your retirement benefit remains with a former employer, keep current on any changes your former employer makes, including changes of address, mergers, or employer name.
- If you move, give the plan your new contact information.

► CHAPTER 9: POTENTIAL CLAIMS AGAINST YOUR BENEFIT (DIVORCE)

In general, your retirement plan is safe from claims by other people. Creditors to whom you owe money cannot make a claim against funds that you have in a retirement plan. For example, if you leave your employer and transfer your **401(k)** account into an **individual retirement account (IRA)**, creditors generally cannot get access to those IRA funds even if you declare bankruptcy.

Federal law does make an exception for family support and the division of property at divorce. A state court can award part or all of a participant's retirement benefit to the spouse, former spouse, child, or other dependent. The recipient named in the order is called the alternate payee. The court issues a specific court order, called a domestic relations order, which can be in the form of a state court judgment, decree or order, or court approval of a property settlement agreement. The order must relate to child support, alimony, or marital property rights, and must be made under state domestic relations law. The **plan administrator** determines if the order is a qualified domestic relations order (QDRO) under the plan's procedures and then notifies the participant and the alternate payee. If the participant is still employed, a QDRO can require payment to the alternate payee to begin on or after the participant's earliest possible retirement age available under the plan. These rules apply to both **defined benefit** and **defined contribution plans**. For additional information, see EBSA's publication, "QDROs – The Division of Retirement Benefits Through Qualified Domestic Relations Orders," available on the website at **www.dol.gov/ebsa**. To order a copy, contact EBSA electronically at **www.askebsa.dol.gov** or call toll free 1-866-444-3272.

ACTION ITEMS
- If you are involved in a divorce, you should discuss these issues with your plan administrator and your attorney.

► Chapter 10: What to Do If You Have a Problem

Sometimes, retirement plan administrators, managers, and others involved with the plan make mistakes. Some examples include:

- ► Your **401(k)** or individual account statement is consistently late or comes at irregular intervals;
- ► Your account balance does not appear to be accurate;
- ► Your employer fails to transmit your contribution to the plan on a timely basis;
- ► Your **plan administrator** does not give or send you a copy of the **Summary Plan Description**; or
- ► Your benefit is calculated incorrectly.

It is important for you to know that you can follow up on any possible mistakes without fear of retribution. Employers are prohibited by law from firing or disciplining employees to avoid paying a benefit, as a reprisal for exercising any of the rights provided under a plan or Federal retirement law (**ERISA**), or for giving information or testimony in any inquiry or proceeding related to ERISA.

Start with your employer and/or plan administrator

If you find an error or have a question, in most cases, you can start by looking for information in your Summary Plan Description. In addition, you can contact your employer and/or the plan administrator and ask them to explain what has happened and/or make a correction.

Is it possible to sue under ERISA?

Yes, you have a right to sue your plan and its **fiduciaries** to enforce or clarify your rights under ERISA and your plan in the following situations:

- ► To appeal a denied claim for benefits after exhausting your plan's claims review process;
- ► To recover benefits due you;
- ► To clarify your right to future benefits;
- ► To obtain plan documents that you previously requested in writing but did not receive;
- ► To address a breach of a plan fiduciary's duties; or
- ► To stop the plan from continuing any act or practice that violates the terms of the plan or ERISA.

What is the role of the Labor Department?

The U.S. Department of Labor's Employee Benefits Security Administration (EBSA) is the agency responsible for enforcing the provisions of ERISA that govern the conduct of plan fiduciaries, the investment and protection of plan assets, the reporting and disclosure of plan information, and participants' benefit rights and responsibilities.

However, not all retirement plans are covered by ERISA. For example, Federal, state, or local government plans and some church plans are not covered.

The Department of Labor enforces the law by informally resolving benefit disputes, conducting investigations, and seeking correction of violations of the law, including bringing lawsuits when necessary.

The Department has benefits advisors committed to providing individual assistance to participants and beneficiaries. Participants will receive information on their rights and responsibilities under the law and help in obtaining benefits to which they are entitled.

Contact a benefits advisor electronically by visiting the website at **www.dol.gov/ebsa** and clicking on "Request Assistance" or by calling toll free 1-866-444-3272.

ACTION ITEMS

Contact the Department of Labor's EBSA for questions about ERISA, help in obtaining a benefit, or:

- ▸ If you believe your claim to benefits has been unjustly denied or that your benefit was calculated incorrectly;
- ▸ If you have information that plan assets are being mismanaged or misused;
- ▸ If you think the plan fiduciaries are acting improperly; or
- ▸ If you think your employer has been late in depositing your contributions (see Chapter 7).

WHAT OTHER FEDERAL AGENCIES CAN ASSIST PARTICIPANTS AND BENEFICIARIES?

The Pension Benefit Guaranty Corporation (PBGC) is a federally created corporation that guarantees payment of certain pension benefits under most private defined benefit plans when they are terminated with insufficient money to pay benefits.

You may contact the PBGC at:
Pension Benefit Guaranty Corporation
1200 K Street, NW
Washington, DC 20005-4026
Tel (202) 326-4000
Toll free 1-800-400-PBGC (7242)
www.pbgc.gov

The Treasury Department's Internal Revenue Service is responsible for the rules that allow tax benefits for both employees and employers related to retirement plans, including vesting and distribution requirements. The IRS maintains a taxpayer assistance line for retirement plans at 1-877-829-5500 (toll-free number). The call center is open Monday through Friday.

▶ GLOSSARY

401(k) Plan – In this type of defined contribution plan, the employee can make contributions from his or her paycheck before taxes are taken out. The contributions go into a 401(k) account, with the employee often choosing the investments based on options provided under the plan. In some plans, the employer also makes contributions, matching the employee's contributions up to a certain percentage. SIMPLE and safe harbor 401(k) plans have additional employer contribution and vesting requirements.

Automatic Enrollment – Employers can automatically enroll employees in a plan, such as a 401(k) or SIMPLE IRA plan, and place contributions deducted from employees' paychecks into certain predetermined investments, unless the employees decide otherwise. Participants have the opportunity to opt out of participation and periodic opportunities to change their investments (or in a SIMPLE IRA, the financial institution where the contributions are invested).

Benefit Accrual – The amount of benefits accumulated under the plan.

Cash Balance Plan – A type of defined benefit plan that includes some elements that are similar to a defined contribution plan because the benefit amount is computed based on a formula using contribution and earning credits, and each participant has a hypothetical account. Cash balance plans are more likely than traditional defined benefit plans to make lump sum distributions. (For more information, see "Frequently Asked Questions about Cash Balance Pension Plans" on the Department of Labor's website, at **www.dol.gov/ebsa/faqs/**.)

Defined Benefit Plan – This type of plan, also known as the traditional pension plan, promises the participant a specified monthly benefit at retirement. Often, the benefit is based on factors such as your salary, your age, and the number of years you worked for the employer.

Defined Contribution Plan – In a defined contribution plan, the employee and/or the employer contribute to the employee's individual account under the plan. The employee often decides how his or her account is invested. The amount in the account at distribution includes the contributions and investment gains or losses, minus any investment and administrative fees. The contributions and earnings are not taxed until distribution. The value of the account will change based on the value and performance of the investments.

Employee Retirement Income Security Act of 1974 (ERISA) – A Federal law that sets standards of protection for individuals in most voluntarily established, private-sector retirement plans. ERISA requires plans to provide participants with plan information, including important facts about plan features and funding; sets minimum standards for participation, vesting, benefit accrual, and funding; provides fiduciary responsibilities for those who manage and control plan assets; requires plans to establish a claims and appeals process for participants to get benefits from their plans; gives participants the right to sue for benefits and breaches of fiduciary duty; and, if a defined benefit plan is terminated, guarantees payment of certain benefits through a Federally chartered corporation, known as the Pension Benefit Guaranty Corporation (PBGC).

Employee Stock Ownership Plan (ESOP) – A type of defined contribution plan that is invested primarily in employer stock.

Individual Benefit Statement – An individual benefit statement provides information about a participant's retirement benefits, such as the total plan benefits earned and vested benefits, on a periodic basis. Additional information may be included depending upon the type of plan, such as how a participant's 401(k) plan account is invested and the value of those investments.

Individual Retirement Account (IRA) – An individual account set up with a financial institution, such as a bank or a mutual fund company. Under Federal law, individuals may set aside personal savings up to a certain amount, and the investments grow, tax deferred. In addition, defined contribution plan participants can transfer money from an employer retirement plan to an IRA when leaving an employer. IRAs also can be part of an employer plan.

Money Purchase Plan – A money purchase plan requires set annual contributions from the employer to individual accounts and is subject to other rules.

Multiemployer Plan – A retirement plan sponsored by several employers under collective bargaining agreements that meets certain other requirements. A participant who changes jobs from one sponsoring employer to another stays within the same plan.

Plan Administrator – The person who is identified in the plan document as having responsibility for running the plan. It could be the employer, a committee of employees, a company executive, or someone hired for that purpose.

Plan Document – A written instrument under which the plan is established and operated.

Plan Fiduciary – Anyone who exercises discretionary authority or discretionary control over management or administration of the plan, exercises any authority or control over management or disposition of plan assets, or gives investment advice for a fee or other compensation with respect to assets of the plan.

Plan Trustee – Someone who has the exclusive authority and discretion to manage and control the assets of the plan. The trustee can be subject to the direction of a named fiduciary and the named fiduciary can appoint one or more investment managers for the plan's assets.

Plan Year – A 12-month period designated by a retirement plan for calculating vesting and distribution, among other things. The plan year can be the calendar year or an alternative period, e.g., July 1 to June 30.

Profit Sharing Plan – A profit sharing plan allows the employer each year to determine how much to contribute to the plan (out of profits or otherwise) in cash or employer stock. The plan contains a formula for allocating the annual contribution among the participants.

Rollover – A rollover occurs when a participant leaves an employer and directs the defined contribution plan to transfer the money in his or her account to a new plan or individual retirement account. This preserves the benefits and does not trigger any tax consequences if done in a timely manner.

Safe Harbor 401(k) – A safe harbor 401(k) is similar to a traditional 401(k) plan, but the employer is required to make contributions for each employee. The employer contributions in safe harbor 401(k) plans are immediately 100 percent vested. The safe harbor 401(k) eases administrative burdens on employers by eliminating some of the complex tax rules ordinarily applied to traditional 401(k) plans.

Savings Incentive Match Plan for Employees of Small Employers (SIMPLE) – A plan in which a small business with 100 or fewer employees can offer retirement benefits through employee salary reductions and matching contributions (similar to those found in a 401(k) plan). It can be either a SIMPLE IRA or a SIMPLE 401(k). SIMPLE IRA plans impose few administrative burdens on employers because IRAs are owned by the employees and the bank or financial institution receiving the funds does most of the paperwork. While each has some different features, including contribution limits and the availability of loans, required employer contributions are immediately 100 percent vested in both.

Simplified Employee Pension Plan (SEP) – A plan in which the employer makes contributions on a tax-favored basis to individual retirement accounts (IRAs) owned by the employees. If certain conditions are met, the employer is not subject to the reporting and disclosure requirements of most retirement plans. Under a SEP, an IRA is set up by or for an employee to accept the employer's contributions.

Summary Plan Description – A document provided by the plan administrator that includes a plain language description of important features of the plan, e.g., when employees begin to participate in the plan, how service and benefits are calculated, when benefits become vested, when payment is received and in what form, and how to file a claim for benefits. Participants must be informed of material changes either through a revised Summary Plan Description or in a separate document called a Summary of Material Modifications.

Vested Benefits – Those benefits that the individual has earned a right to receive and that cannot be forfeited.

Years of Service – The time an individual has worked in a job covered by the plan. It is used to determine when an individual can participate and vest and how they can accrue benefits in the plan.

www.ingramcontent.com/pod-product-compliance
Lightning Source LLC
Chambersburg PA
CBHW080923290526
45795CB00007BA/2636